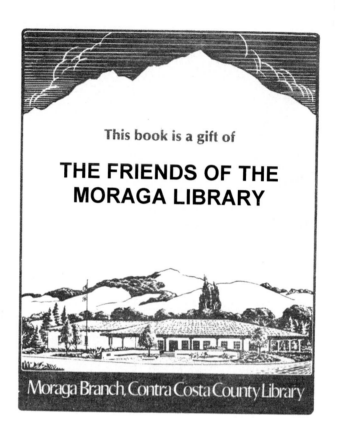

THE BEST MLB
TEAMS
OF ALL TIME

By Alex Monnig

Published by ABDO Publishing Company, PO Box 398166, Minneapolis,
MN 55439. Copyright © 2014 by Abdo Consulting Group, Inc.
International copyrights reserved in all countries. No part of this book
may be reproduced in any form without written permission from the
publisher. SportsZone™ is a trademark and logo of ABDO Publishing
Company.

Printed in the United States of America,
North Mankato, Minnesota
102013
012014

Editor: Chrös McDougall
Series Designer: Christa Schneider

Photo credits: AP Images, cover (background), 1 (background), 7, 9,
13, 15, 17, 21, 23, 25, 27, 29, 31, 33, 35, 37, 39, 41, 43, 45, 47; Charles
Krupa/AP Images, cover, 1; National Baseball Library, Cooperstown,
N.Y./AP Images, 11; Murrary Becker/AP Images, 19; Harry Cabluck/AP
Images, 49; Ed Reinke/AP Images, 51, 53; Elise Amendola/AP Images,
55; Mark J. Terrill/AP Images, 57; Kathy Willens/AP Images, 59; Amy
Sancetta/AP Images, 61

Library of Congress Control Number: 2013945886

Cataloging-in-Publication Data
Monnig, Alex.
 The best MLB teams of all time / Alex Monnig.
   p. cm. -- (Major League Baseball's best ever)
Includes bibliographical references and index.
ISBN 978-1-62403-118-2
1. Major League Baseball (Organization)--Juvenile literature. 2. Baseball
teams--Juvenile literature.   I. Title.
796.357--dc23

                                                      2013945886

TABLE OF CONTENTS

INTRODUCTION

There are great teams. And then there are teams that live forever in history.

In Major League Baseball (MLB) history, a few teams stand above the rest. Some are memorable because they simply dominated. They entertained fans all season long. Others are remembered for shocking the baseball world. When nobody expected it, they came in and won. And some teams are remembered for simply putting on a show. They made every game interesting. And ultimately these teams usually came out on top. Win or lose, they entertained millions of baseball fans throughout the summer and fall.

Here are some of the best teams in MLB history.

1907 CHICAGO CUBS

The 1906 Chicago Cubs won 116 games.
Through 2013, no team had won more. But the 1907
Cubs achieved something the 1906 squad could not.
They won the World Series.

The core of Chicago's 1906 team returned in
1907. And those players were motivated to finish what
they had started. The Cubs rolled through the regular
season with 107 wins. That was 15 more than the next-
best team in baseball. They met the Detroit Tigers
in the World Series. The teams tied the first game.
Then Chicago swept the next four to win the title.
Mission accomplished.

Pitching led the way all year for Chicago. No
pitching staff gave up fewer hits or fewer earned runs.

Chicago Cubs infielders Joe Tinker, *left*, and Johnny Evers
helped the team win 107 games and the World Series in 1907.

Mordecai "Three Finger" Brown was the staff ace. He had lost part of a finger during a farming accident. But the true victims of the injury ended up being the hitters he faced from the mound.

"The old paw served me pretty well," Brown said. "It gave me a firmer grip on the ball, so I could spin it over the hump. It gave me a greater dip."

Cubs pitchers had another secret weapon. In fact, they had three: first baseman Frank Chance, second baseman Johnny Evers, and shortstop Joe Tinker. The trio was so good that it became part of a popular poem called "Baseball's Sad Lexicon." In the poem, the author describes the three Cubs turning double plays.

The Cubs did not get a lot of hits or home runs. But pitching and defense made up for middle-of-the-pack hitting. The Cubs also walked a lot and rarely struck out. And that was enough.

5

The number of 1907 Cubs pitchers who ranked in the top seven in earned-run average (ERA) in baseball that year.

M. BROWN. J. PFEISTER A. HOFMAN C.G. WILLIAMS O. OVERALL. E. REULBACH. J. KLING.
SSLER. J. TAYLOR. H. STEINFELDT. J. McCORMICK. F. CHANCE. J. SHECKARD. P. MORAN. F. SCH
C. LUNDGREN. T. WALSH. J. EVERS. J. SLAGLE. J. TINKER.

Several players from the great 1906 Chicago Cubs returned to help the team win the World Series one year later.

1907 CHICAGO CUBS

KEY STATS AND PLAYERS

Record: 107–45

Postseason: Won World Series over the Detroit Tigers 4–0–1

Mordecai Brown

Position: Pitcher

Age: 30

Key Stat: 20 wins

Orval Overall

Position: Pitcher

Age: 26

Key Stat: 8 shutouts

Johnny Evers

Position: Second Baseman

Age: 25

Key Stat: 46 stolen bases

Jack Pfeister

Position: Pitcher

Age: 29

Key Stat: 1.15 ERA

1927 NEW YORK YANKEES

The New York Yankees are the unquestioned kings of baseball. Through 2013, they had won 27 World Series, more than double the next best team. And of all those great Yankees teams, perhaps none was better than the 1927 version.

Those Yankees featured a lineup so good that it became known as "Murderer's Row." Four Hall of Fame players made up the heart of the order. Outfielder Earle Combs and second baseman Tony Lazzeri were great. Outfielder Babe Ruth and first baseman Lou Gehrig were legendary.

Many cite Ruth as the greatest player of all time. And he was at his best in 1927. In an era before home runs were common, Ruth hit 60. That was a record that stood for more than three decades.

"The Bambino" Babe Ruth was in his prime while helping the New York Yankees win the 1927 World Series.

Ruth had won the American League (AL) Most Valuable Player (MVP) Award in 1923. He might have won again, but previous winners were not eligible at the time. Instead, Gehrig took the award. The dependable first baseman hit .373 with 47 home runs and 175 runs batted in (RBIs). After Ruth and Gehrig, the next best home run total in the AL was Lazzeri's 18.

The Yankees certainly had power. They also had pitching. The Yankees gave up the fewest runs in the majors. Hall of Fame pitcher Waite Hoyt tied for the AL lead with 22 wins. And Wilcy Moore, Hoyt, and Urban Shocker finished one-two-three in ERA.

Even manager Miller Huggins was a Hall of Famer. So it was hardly a surprise that the Yankees won—a lot. They breezed through the AL with a 110–44 record. Then they swept the Pittsburgh Pirates in the World Series.

12

The number of teams that hit fewer than Ruth's record-setting 60 home runs in 1927. MLB had 16 teams in 1927.

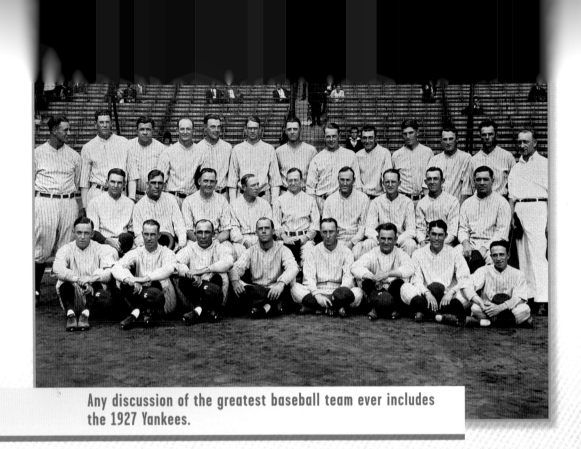

Any discussion of the greatest baseball team ever includes the 1927 Yankees.

1927 NEW YORK YANKEES

KEY STATS AND PLAYERS

Record: 110–44

Postseason: Won World Series over the Pittsburgh Pirates 4–0

Earle Combs

Position: Outfielder

Age: 28

Key Stat: 231 hits

Lou Gehrig

Position: First Baseman

Age: 24

Key Stat: .373 batting average

Waite Hoyt

Position: Pitcher

Age: 27

Key Stat: 22 wins

Babe Ruth

Position: Outfielder

Age: 32

Key Stat: 60 home runs

1929 PHILADELPHIA ATHLETICS

From 1929 to 1931, no team dominated like the Philadelphia Athletics. They made it to three straight World Series, winning twice. But the 1929 squad stood above the rest.

Leading the team was legendary manager Connie Mack. He managed the A's for 50 seasons and won more games than any other manager. His 1929 batting order featured a two-headed power monster of young first baseman Jimmie Foxx and outfielder Al Simmons. They hit a combined 67 home runs that season. And Simmons led the AL with 157 RBIs.

The A's were deep, too. An amazing six different regular starters hit better than .310. One of those starters was catcher Mickey Cochrane. He helped manage a dominant pitching staff.

From left, Jimmy Foxx, Mickey Cochrane, and Al Simmons led the 1929 Philadelphia Athletics into baseball immortality.

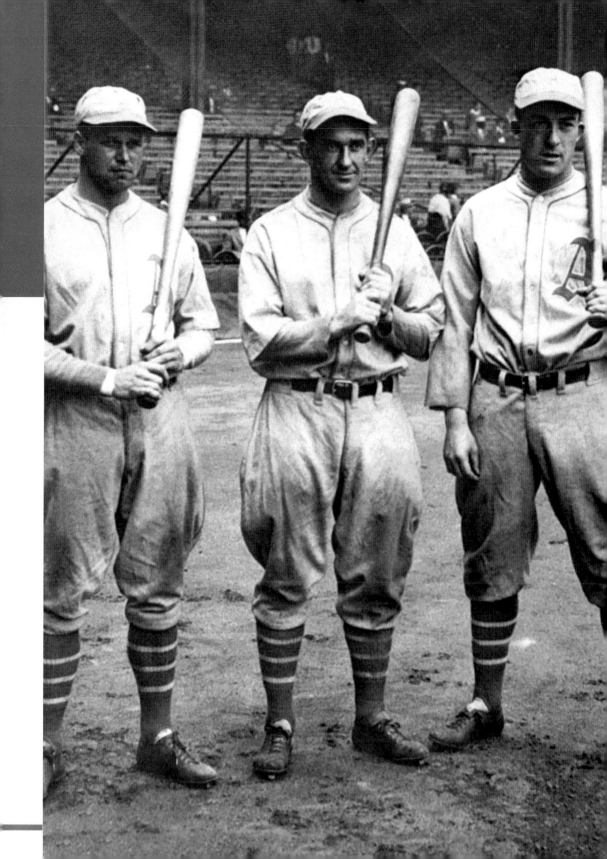

Staff ace Lefty Grove hardly needed help, though. The Hall of Famer was one of the greatest pitchers of all time. And in 1929, he led all of baseball with a 2.81 ERA. Meanwhile, pitcher George Earnshaw's 24 wins were the best in baseball.

313

The number of A's wins from 1929 to 1931. That was the most of any team during that span.

However, Mack decided to start 35-year-old Howard Ehmke in Game 1 of the World Series against the Chicago Cubs. Players from both teams were shocked. But it proved to be a genius move. Ehmke's loopy curveball moved away from the right-handed hitters. That pitch helped him record 13 strikeouts in a 3–1 A's victory. Philadelphia went on to win four games to one.

"Perhaps the 1927 Yankees were the greatest team of all time," *Washington Post* sports editor Shirley Povich said years later. "But if there was a close second, perhaps an equal, it was those A's. They are the most overlooked team in baseball."

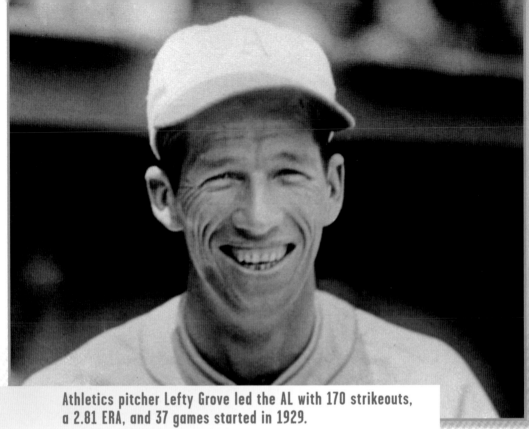

Athletics pitcher Lefty Grove led the AL with 170 strikeouts, a 2.81 ERA, and 37 games started in 1929.

1929 PHILADELPHIA ATHLETICS

KEY STATS AND PLAYERS

Record: 104–46

Postseason: Won World Series over the Chicago Cubs 4–1

George Earnshaw

Position: Pitcher

Age: 29

Key Stat: 24 wins

Lefty Grove

Position: Pitcher

Age: 29

Key Stat: 170 strikeouts

Jimmie Foxx

Position: First Baseman

Age: 21

Key Stat: 33 home runs

Al Simmons

Position: Outfielder

Age: 27

Key Stat: 157 RBIs

1939
NEW YORK YANKEES

Thousands of fans showed up at Yankee Stadium on July 4, 1939. A mysterious disease had stricken New York Yankees legend Lou Gehrig. It forced him to retire. So he stood in front of the crowd to say goodbye.

Joe DiMaggio also was in the stadium that day. And the outfielder known as "Joltin' Joe" was ready to follow in Gehrig's footsteps as the next Yankees legend.

DiMaggio won the first of his three MVP Awards in 1939. He led the majors with a .381 batting average. Meanwhile, third baseman Red Rolfe led all of baseball with 213 hits and 139 runs. All in all, the Yankees had four players with 100-plus runs and four players with 100-plus RBIs.

New York Yankees legend Lou Gehrig says goodbye to the home fans on July 4, 1939, at Yankee Stadium.

Throughout the season, the Yankees hit well. Then they kept hitting. Then they hit some more. Their 967 runs scored were 77 more than the second-place Boston Red Sox. The Yankees outscored their opponents by a whopping 411 runs.

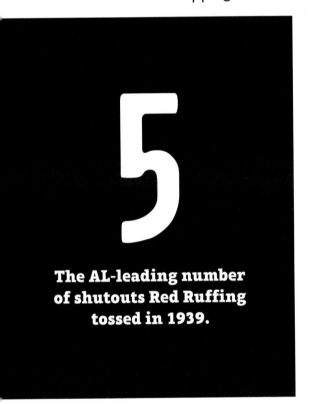

5

The AL-leading number of shutouts Red Ruffing tossed in 1939.

Great pitching certainly helped. Pitchers Red Ruffing and Monte Pearson led the way for New York. Behind them, the Yankees allowed the fewest runs in baseball.

The great hitting and great pitching guided New York to a 106–45 record. The powerful pitching staff then carried the Yankees to a World Series sweep. The Cincinnati Reds were only able to score eight runs in the four losses. With the win, the Yankees had claimed four World Series in a row. No team in MLB history had done that. And behind DiMaggio, they were not done winning World Series.

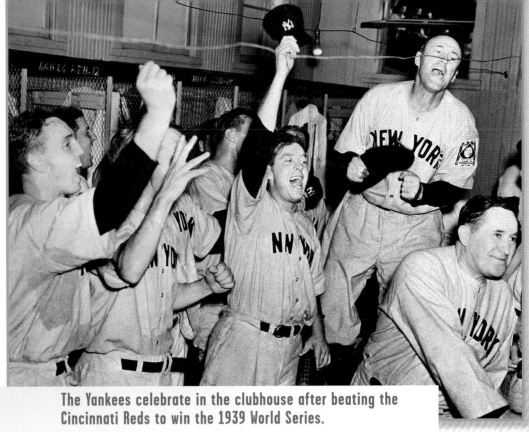

The Yankees celebrate in the clubhouse after beating the Cincinnati Reds to win the 1939 World Series.

1939 NEW YORK YANKEES

KEY STATS AND PLAYERS

Record: 106–45

Postseason: Won World Series over the Cincinnati Reds 4–0

Joe DiMaggio
Position: Outfielder
Age: 24
Key Stat: .381 batting average

Red Rolfe
Position: Third Baseman
Age: 30
Key Stat: 213 hits

Joe Gordon
Position: Second Baseman
Age: 24
Key Stat: 28 home runs

Red Ruffing
Position: Pitcher
Age: 34
Key Stat: 21 wins

1942
ST. LOUIS
CARDINALS

Fifty-three games remained in the 1942 season. The St. Louis Cardinals trailed the Brooklyn Dodgers by 10 games. Any chance of a pennant appeared slim. But with a 44–7 run to end the season, the Cardinals beat the odds. They won the NL pennant by two games.

The Cardinals kept flying in the World Series. The opposing New York Yankees had won five of the past six championships. But St. Louis took the 1942 title in five games.

The "Cardiac Cardinals" relied on good pitching to overcome a lack of stars at the plate. Pitcher Mort Cooper led all of baseball with a 1.78 ERA and tied for the lead with 22 wins. That earned him the NL MVP Award. Meanwhile, pitcher Johnny Beazley had 21 wins. And as a staff, the Cardinals led the majors in ERA.

St. Louis' Whitey Kurowski, *left*, Enos Slaughter, *center*, and Johnny Beazley celebrate the 1942 World Series championship.

"Country" Enos Slaughter and rookie Stan "The Man" Musial led the Cardinals' offense. The outfielders were the only two everyday players to hit better than .300. They also were the only two Cardinals to hit more than 10 home runs. The team only had 60 in total.

Musial blossomed into a superstar in 1943. In 1942, he was just a 21-year-old rookie with a quirky, coiled batting stance. But even though he didn't have much power in 1942, he found a way to get the job done, just as the Cardinals did.

"In '42, we played together and fought together," Musial said. "We had that Cardinal spirit; we thought we could beat anybody and we did. We fought tooth and nail."

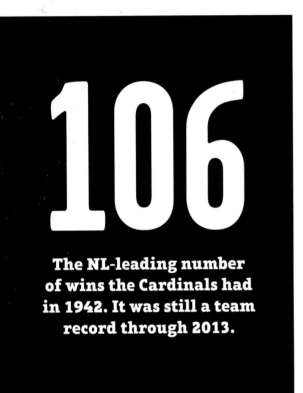

106

The NL-leading number of wins the Cardinals had in 1942. It was still a team record through 2013.

From left, Ray Sanders, Enos Slaughter, and Stan Musial helped the "Cardiac Cardinals" win 106 games in 1942.

1942 ST. LOUIS CARDINALS
KEY STATS AND PLAYERS

Record: 106–48

Postseason: Won World Series over the New York Yankees 4–1

Johnny Beazley
Position: Pitcher
Age: 24
Key Stat: 21 wins

Mort Cooper
Position: Pitcher
Age: 29
Key Stat: 1.78 ERA

Stan Musial
Position: Outfielder
Age: 21
Key Stat: .315 batting average

Enos Slaughter
Position: Outfielder
Age: 26
Key Stat: 188 hits

1954
CLEVELAND
INDIANS

Baseball's original "Dead-Ball Era" came in the early 1900s. It was named so because hitters hardly stood a chance against the awesome pitchers of the time. In 1954, the Cleveland Indians' hurlers led a mini dead-ball era of their own.

Cleveland pitchers Early Wynn, Bob Lemon, Bob Feller, and Hal Newhouser all were later enshrined in the Hall of Fame. In 1954, Wynn and Lemon tied with one other player for the MLB lead with 23 wins. Wynn, Lemon, and Mike Garcia all had top-five ERAs.

It didn't hurt that Indians second baseman Bobby Avila led the AL with a .341 batting average. And outfielder Larry Doby paced the league with 32 home runs and 126 RBIs. Doby was the first black player in the AL.

Bob Feller warms up while 1954 Cleveland Indians teammates, *from left*, Mike Garcia, Bob Lemon, and Early Wynn look on.

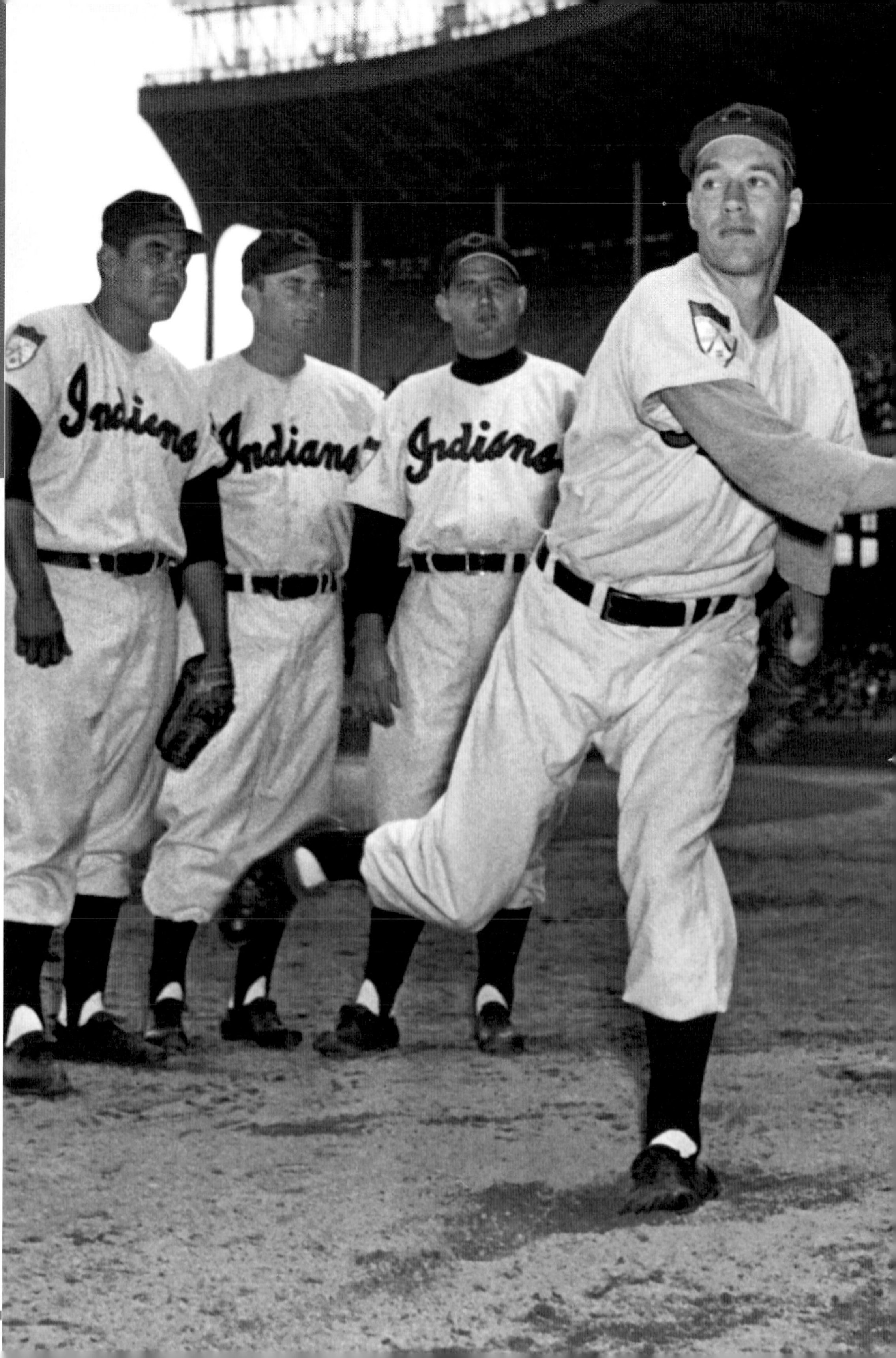
Indians
Indians
Indians

Those performances helped the Indians end another run of dominance by the New York Yankees. The Yankees came into that season having won five straight World Series from 1949 to 1953. They then won 103 games in 1954. But they could only dream of a sixth World Series as the season came to a close. That is because the Indians won an amazing 111 games, clinching the AL pennant. There were no playoffs at the time.

But the high-flying performances in the regular season were nowhere to be found in the World Series. The New York Giants averaged more than five runs per game against the Indians. Meanwhile, Cleveland could only push nine runs total across home plate. The Giants swept the series. And the 1954 Indians went down as one of the best teams to miss out on a championship.

156

The AL-leading number of home runs the Indians hit in 1954.

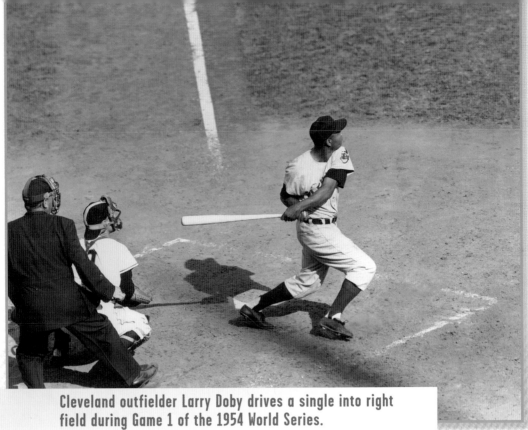

Cleveland outfielder Larry Doby drives a single into right field during Game 1 of the 1954 World Series.

1954 CLEVELAND INDIANS

KEY STATS AND PLAYERS

Record: 111–43

Postseason: Lost World Series to the New York Giants 4–0

Larry Doby
Position: Outfielder
Age: 30
Key Stat: 32 home runs

Bob Lemon
Position: Pitcher
Age: 33
Key Stat: 23 wins

Mike Garcia
Position: Pitcher
Age: 30
Key Stat: 2.64 ERA

Early Wynn
Position: Pitcher
Age: 34
Key Stat: 155 strikeouts

1961
NEW YORK YANKEES

They called them the "M&M Boys."

Mickey Mantle was the rock star. He was one of the most exciting and popular players in the game. The switch-hitter crushed towering home runs that flew over the wall. Roger Maris was quieter and not as celebrated. But he hit home runs, too. And together the two outfielders helped make the 1961 New York Yankees one of the most popular teams of all time.

The M&M Boys were neck and neck all year at the top of the home run leader board. Together they hit 115 home runs that season. No two teammates had surpassed that in one season through 2013. In the end, it was Maris who came out on top. He hit 61 home runs that season. That broke Babe Ruth's legendary record of 60 set in 1927. Mantle ended the season with 54.

Roger Maris, *left*, and Mickey Mantle—the "M&M Boys"—led the New York Yankees to the 1961 World Series title.

The Yankees had a record-setter on the mound, too. Hall of Famer Whitey Ford won more games than any other Yankees pitcher through 2013. In 1961, he led the majors with 25 wins. Ford also had 209 strikeouts. Yankees pitcher Bill Stafford finished second in baseball with a 2.68 ERA. And closer Luis Arroyo led the MLB with 29 saves.

In total, the Yankees had eight AL All-Stars that season. They combined to lead New York to 109 wins and a World Series victory over the Cincinnati Reds. The Yankees played in the World Series each year from 1960 to 1964. The 1961 squad stands out, though. That year will always be remembered for the home run battle between the M&M Boys.

5

The number of players who had hit at least 54 home runs in a season before Mantle and Maris did it in 1961.

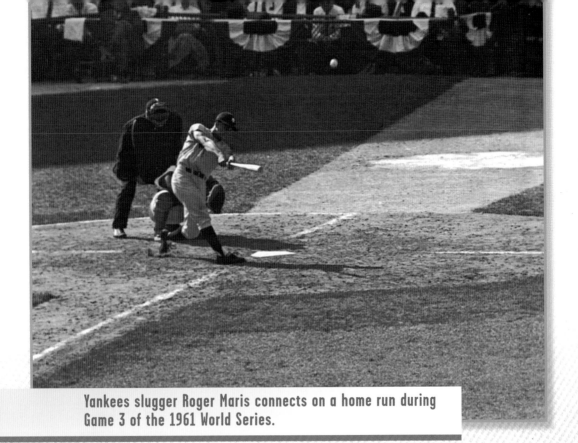

Yankees slugger Roger Maris connects on a home run during Game 3 of the 1961 World Series.

1961 NEW YORK YANKEES

KEY STATS AND PLAYERS

Record: 109–53

Postseason: Won World Series over the Cincinnati Reds 4–1

Whitey Ford

Position: Pitcher

Age: 32

Key Stat: 25 wins

Mickey Mantle

Position: Outfielder

Age: 29

Key Stat: 54 home runs

Roger Maris

Position: Outfielder

Age: 26

Key Stat: 61 home runs

Bill Stafford

Position: Pitcher

Age: 21

Key Stat: 2.68 ERA

1965
LOS ANGELES DODGERS

Only two NL teams scored fewer runs in 1965 than the Los Angeles Dodgers.
Their 78 home runs were the fewest in baseball. But they were the last team standing at the end of the season. The 1965 Dodgers were the first West Coast team to be crowned World Series champion.

The Dodgers did it with speed and pitching. But they almost did not do it at all. Los Angeles was in a tight pennant race. The Dodgers won 15 of their final 16 games to hold off the rival San Francisco Giants. Then they needed to go the full seven games to beat the Minnesota Twins in the World Series.

"We didn't tear the cover off the ball, but we didn't need to because we had players who each contributed in their own way," catcher Jeff Torborg said.

Los Angeles Dodgers pitcher Sandy Koufax throws against the Minnesota Twins in Game 7 of the 1965 World Series.

He added: "We were smart and ran the bases extremely well. We made things happen, and of course it didn't hurt to have two future Hall of Famers going out to the mound every four days."

Sandy Koufax and Don Drysdale were the Hall of Fame pitchers. The left-handed Koufax led the majors in wins (26), strikeouts (382), and complete games (27) that season. He even pitched a perfect game right in the heart of the pennant race. It was no wonder he won the Cy Young Award. It was given to the best pitcher in the majors until 1967. Today the award is given to the best pitcher in each league. Drysdale added 23 wins and 20 complete games of his own that season.

2

The number of games the 1965 Dodgers won in which they had just one hit.

The Dodgers did not have a superstar hitter. But they sure knew how to steal bases. Shortstop Maury Wills led the majors with 94 stolen bases. That was 31 more than anybody else.

The Dodgers' Don Drysdale celebrates with Lou Johnson, *left*, and Wes Parker, *right*, after Game 4 of the 1965 World Series.

1965 LOS ANGELES DODGERS

KEY STATS AND PLAYERS

Record: 97–65

Postseason: Won World Series over the Minnesota Twins 4–3

Don Drysdale	**Claude Osteen**
Position: Pitcher	**Position:** Pitcher
Age: 28	**Age:** 25
Key Stat: 23 wins	**Key Stat:** 2.79 ERA
Sandy Koufax	**Maury Wills**
Position: Pitcher	**Position:** Shortstop
Age: 29	**Age:** 32
Key Stat: 382 strikeouts	**Key Stat:** 94 stolen bases

1969
NEW YORK
METS

For the longest time they were miserable. Then in 1969, they were "Amazin'."

The New York Mets debuted in 1962. They finished last or second-to-last in the NL in their first seven seasons. Then they came out of nowhere in 1969 to win 100 games and capture the World Series title.

The "Amazin' Mets," as they came to be known, did it with excellent pitching and stellar defense. Star pitcher Tom Seaver earned the NL Cy Young Award. He had a 25–7 record with a 2.21 ERA and 208 strikeouts. However, he was the only future Hall of Fame player to have a major role on the team. The Mets lacked a superstar on offense. But a different player seemed to step up each night.

New York Mets ace Tom Seaver pitches during Game 4 of the 1969 World Series.

That is what happened in the World Series, too. The opposing Baltimore Orioles were tough. They had a star-studded pitching staff and great hitters. Those players would lead the Orioles back to the World Series in 1970 and 1971. Needless to say, the Mets were underdogs. But that is how they liked it.

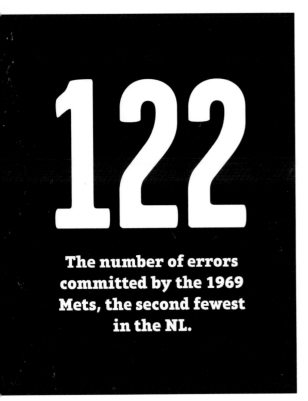

122

The number of errors committed by the 1969 Mets, the second fewest in the NL.

"I've got 25 men outside who think they can win, and that's all that matters," manager Gil Hodges told his son before Game 1.

And win they did. Ron Swoboda was not known for his defense. But in Game 4, he made a diving backhanded catch to turn a potential two-run hit into a sacrifice fly. First baseman Donn Clendenon had been traded twice in 1969. But he stepped up and hit .357 with three home runs to be named World Series MVP. Pretty "Amazin'" for a team nobody thought had a chance.

Fans rush onto the field at Shea Stadium in New York to celebrate the Amazin' Mets' 1969 World Series win.

1969 NEW YORK METS

KEY STATS AND PLAYERS

Record: 100–62

Postseason: Won World Series over the Baltimore Orioles 4–1

Tommie Agee

Position: Outfielder

Age: 26

Key Stat: 26 home runs

Cleon Jones

Position: Outfielder

Age: 26

Key Stat: .340 batting average

Jerry Koosman

Position: Pitcher

Age: 26

Key Stat: 2.28 ERA

Tom Seaver

Position: Pitcher

Age: 24

Key Stat: 25 wins

1970 BALTIMORE ORIOLES

The Baltimore Orioles failed to capture the 1969 World Series. So they were not about to be denied again in 1970.

Hall of Fame manager Earl Weaver helped the team get back to "The Oriole Way" by detailing a step-by-step system for players to follow. It helped Baltimore beat teams in a variety of ways.

"The Oriole Way was never beat yourself," catcher Elrod Hendricks said. "And that's why we won so many close games. We let the other team make mistakes and beat themselves, and when the opportunity came we'd jump on it."

At the plate, Baltimore scored an AL-leading 792 runs. First baseman Boog Powell smacked 35 home runs and tallied 114 RBIs to win the MVP Award.

Baltimore Orioles pitcher Mike Cuellar, *left*, and third baseman Brooks Robinson celebrate the team's 1970 World Series win.

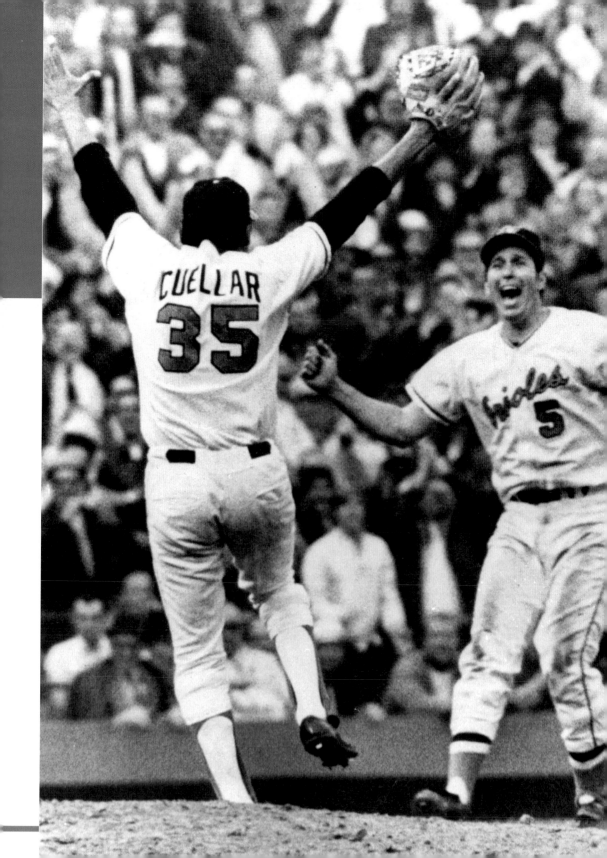

Powell was joined in the lineup by third baseman Brooks Robinson and right fielder Frank Robinson. Both ended up in the Hall of Fame.

But the 1970 Orioles might be best known for their outstanding pitching staff. They led the majors with a 3.15 ERA. Dave McNally, Mike Cuellar, and Jim Palmer all finished in the top five in Cy Young voting. Cuellar and McNally each had 24 wins. That tied with another player for the most wins in baseball. And Palmer, with his trademark high leg kick and smooth delivery, led the AL with a 2.71 ERA.

Baltimore cruised to the AL East pennant by a whopping 15 games. Then the Orioles swept the Minnesota Twins in three games to reach the World Series. Baltimore came out on top in their second of three consecutive World Series appearances. They beat the Cincinnati Reds in five games.

3

The number of 1970 Orioles (Boog Powell, Brooks Robinson, and Frank Robinson) that finished in the top 10 in AL MVP voting.

Baltimore first baseman Boog Powell blasts a home run against the Cincinnati Reds during the 1970 World Series.

1970 BALTIMORE ORIOLES

KEY STATS AND PLAYERS

Record: 108–54

Postseason: Won World Series over the Cincinnati Reds 4–1

Mike Cuellar	**Jim Palmer**
Position: Pitcher	**Position:** Pitcher
Age: 33	**Age:** 24
Key Stat: 24 wins	**Key Stat:** 2.71 ERA
Dave McNally	**Boog Powell**
Position: Pitcher	**Position:** First Baseman
Age: 27	**Age:** 28
Key Stat: 24 wins	**Key Stat:** 35 home runs

1975

CINCINNATI REDS

Opposing pitchers saw a trend when facing the Cincinnati Reds of the early 1970s. Like clockwork, the Reds would go through their batting order and never seem to slow down. They were so effective that they became known as the "Big Red Machine." And in 1975, the machine was firing on all cylinders.

The Reds' lineup featured three Hall of Famers. Pete Rose finished his career as baseball's all-time hits leader. Johnny Bench is arguably the best hitting catcher of all time. He clubbed 28 home runs that year. And first baseman Tony Perez added 20 home runs.

The team was not all about the power, though. Rose was nicknamed "Charlie Hustle" because of his full-speed style of play. That helped him get 210 hits. And the Reds' best all-around player was NL MVP Joe Morgan.

Cincinnati Reds catcher Johnny Bench hits a two-run homer during Game 3 of the 1975 World Series.

Morgan hit .327 with 17 homers, 94 RBIs, and 67 stolen bases.

Cincinnati was spectacular in the field, too. Bench, Morgan, shortstop Dave Concepcion, and outfielder Cesar Geronimo won Gold Gloves that season. And the Reds' pitching staff finished with the third-best ERA in the NL.

That year, the Reds outclassed every other team in baseball. They finished with 108 wins. That was 10 more than any other team. Cincinnati did not run into trouble until the World Series. But even then, the Reds still managed to outlast the pesky Boston Red Sox in seven games.

"[Manager] Sparky Anderson made sure that . . . everybody on the team knew that we were only a little small spoke in the wheel," Morgan said years later. "We weren't the wheel. Everybody here is part of this wheel. . . . He just said, 'Get it done.' And we did."

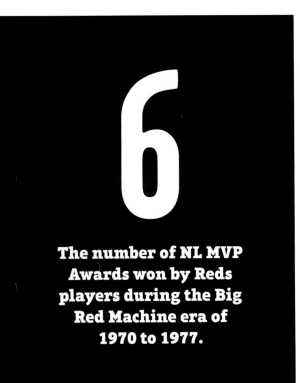

6

The number of NL MVP Awards won by Reds players during the Big Red Machine era of 1970 to 1977.

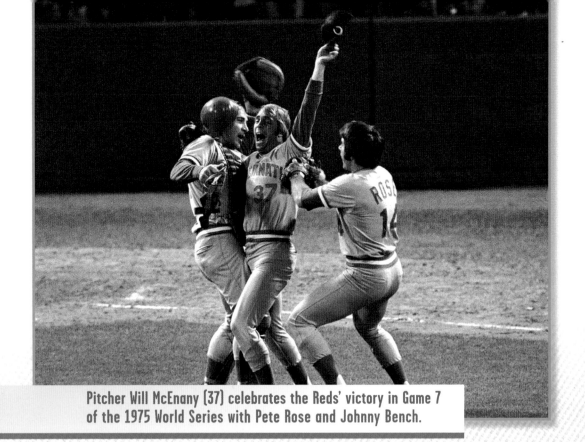

Pitcher Will McEnany (37) celebrates the Reds' victory in Game 7 of the 1975 World Series with Pete Rose and Johnny Bench.

1975 CINCINNATI REDS
KEY STATS AND PLAYERS

Record: 108–54

Postseason: Won World Series over the Boston Red Sox 4–3

Johnny Bench	**Tony Perez**
Position: Catcher	**Position:** First Baseman
Age: 27	**Age:** 33
Key Stat: 28 home runs	**Key Stat:** 109 RBIs
Joe Morgan	**Pete Rose**
Position: Second Baseman	**Position:** Third Baseman
Age: 31	**Age:** 34
Key Stat: 67 stolen bases	**Key Stat:** 210 hits

1995
ATLANTA
BRAVES

The Atlanta Braves had a historically dominant pitching staff during the early 1990s. They had been one of the best teams in baseball, too. But they could not quite take that final step in the postseason until the 1995 season.

Atlanta had lost the 1991 and 1992 World Series. Then it lost in the 1993 playoffs. The 1994 World Series was cancelled due to a players' strike. But everything finally came together in the strike-shortened 1995 season. The Braves led the NL with 90 wins. Then they overcame the Cleveland Indians to win the World Series. Atlanta had its pitching to thank for the success.

Starters Greg Maddux, John Smoltz, and Tom Glavine headlined an elite pitching staff. Atlanta's 3.44 team ERA led the majors for the third year in a row (not including the shortened 1994 season). That was the first time that had been done since 1972.

The Atlanta Braves celebrate after beating the Cleveland Indians in six games in the 1995 World Series.

Maddux won the Cy Young Award for the fourth consecutive year. That was an unheard of accomplishment. He was not a hard thrower. Instead, he relied on his smarts and pinpoint control to get hitters out. Smoltz, on the other hand, could blow his fastball or slider by right-handed hitters and fool lefties with his split-finger pitch.

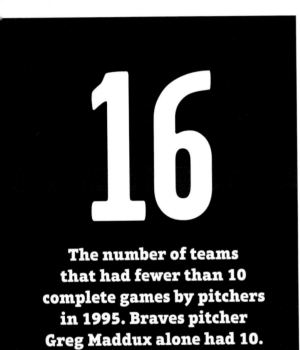

16

The number of teams that had fewer than 10 complete games by pitchers in 1995. Braves pitcher Greg Maddux alone had 10.

The above-average pitching made up for the Braves' mediocre offense. Atlanta's 31 one-run victories led all of baseball. This was perfectly exhibited in the final game of the postseason. It was Game 6 of the World Series. Glavine and reliever Mark Wohlers combined to allow just one hit. So even though the Braves scored just one run, it was enough. They won 1–0. And they were finally champions.

Greg Maddux throws to the plate during the 1995 playoffs.

1995 ATLANTA BRAVES
KEY STATS AND PLAYERS

Record: 90–54

Postseason: Won World Series over the Cleveland Indians 4–2

Tom Glavine	Fred McGriff
Position: Pitcher	**Position:** First Baseman
Age: 29	**Age:** 31
Key Stat: 16 wins	**Key Stat:** 27 home runs
Greg Maddux	John Smoltz
Position: Pitcher	**Position:** Pitcher
Age: 29	**Age:** 28
Key Stat: 1.63 ERA	**Key Stat:** 193 strikeouts

1998
NEW YORK YANKEES

It is not easy to set a New York Yankees team record. So when the 1998 squad won a team-record 114 games, it was a big deal.

By the time they had swept the San Diego Padres in the World Series, the Yankees had 125 total wins. They also had scored more runs than any other team that season and allowed the fewest runs in the AL.

Experienced players provided the leadership. Outfielder Bernie Williams led the AL with a .339 batting average. Pitchers David Wells and David Cone finished third and fourth, respectively, in Cy Young voting. After opening the season 1–4, it was Cone who rallied the team to action.

New York Yankees pitcher Orlando "El Duque" Hernandez winds up to pitch during Game 2 of the 1998 World Series.

But the experienced Yankees could not have done it without help from a younger generation of players. Shortstop Derek Jeter led the AL in runs that season. Catcher Jorge Posada and closer Mariano Rivera would also go on to become Yankees legends. Their timely hitting and pitching was already on display in 1998.

However, down two games to one to the Cleveland Indians in the ALCS, New York turned to an unlikely source. Orlando *"El Duque"* Hernandez had pitched in his native Cuba for years. But he was an MLB rookie. He jokingly waited tables in the team's hotel with a big smile on his face the morning of Game 4. Then he went out and pitched seven shutout innings that night. The Yankees won the next six games to capture the World Series, cementing their place as one of the best teams of all time.

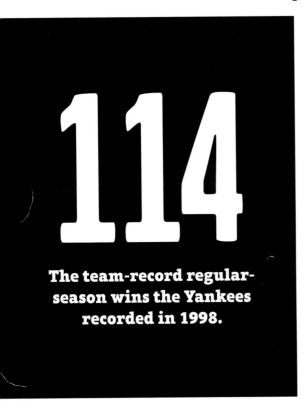

114

The team-record regular-season wins the Yankees recorded in 1998.

The Yankees celebrate after beating the San Diego Padres to win the 1998 World Series.

1998 NEW YORK YANKEES

KEY STATS AND PLAYERS

Record: 114–48

Postseason: Won World Series over the San Diego Padres 4–0

David Cone	**David Wells**
Position: Pitcher	**Position:** Pitcher
Age: 35	**Age:** 35
Key Stat: 209 strikeouts	**Key Stat:** 18 wins
Derek Jeter	**Bernie Williams**
Position: Shortstop	**Position:** Outfielder
Age: 24	**Age:** 29
Key Stat: 127 runs	**Key Stat:** .339 batting average

BOSTON
RED SOX

The Boston Red Sox had not won a World Series since 1918. But "a bunch of idiots" managed to change that in historic fashion.

The 2004 Red Sox were free spirits. They were known for playing jokes on each other. That led one player to refer to the squad as "a bunch of idiots." That attitude might have helped when Boston went down 3–0 to the rival New York Yankees in the ALCS. No team had ever come back from that deficit in a postseason series. But the Red Sox did. They won the next four games over the Yankees. Then they swept the St. Louis Cardinals to claim the World Series title.

Two of the biggest goofballs on the team were outfielder Manny Ramirez and designated hitter David Ortiz. They finished third and fourth, respectively, in AL MVP voting.

Boston Red Sox pitcher Curt Schilling fires to the plate against the New York Yankees during the 2004 ALCS.

On the mound, Pedro Martinez and Curt Schilling finished second and third, respectively, in the AL in strikeouts. They also finished in the top four in Cy Young voting.

Schilling was known as a postseason warrior. That showed in Game 6 of the ALCS. A surgically repaired right ankle injury started bleeding through his sock. But that did not stop him from allowing just one run in seven innings.

The epic comeback required contributions from superstars and role players alike. Utility man Kevin Millar said it was the team's closeness that made it possible.

"Those kinds of things you can't teach," he said. "You either have it or you don't. We had the right mix. We loved each other. It's hard to explain, but we cared because there were good guys."

949

The number of runs the 2004 Red Sox scored—52 more than the next-highest total in baseball.

Red Sox slugger David Ortiz rounds first base after hitting the game-winning home run in Game 4 of the 2004 ALCS.

2004 BOSTON RED SOX

KEY STATS AND PLAYERS

Record: 98–64

Postseason: Won World Series over the St. Louis Cardinals 4–0

Pedro Martinez	**Manny Ramirez**
Position: Pitcher	**Position:** Outfielder
Age: 32	**Age:** 32
Key Stat: 227 strikeouts	**Key Stat:** 43 home runs
David Ortiz	**Curt Schilling**
Position: Designated Hitter	**Position:** Pitcher
Age: 28	**Age:** 37
Key Stat: 139 RBIs	**Key Stat:** 21 wins

HONORABLE MENTIONS

1902 Pittsburgh Pirates (103–36) – If the World Series had existed, they probably would have won it. The Pirates never lost more than two games in a row all season.

1906 Chicago Cubs (116–36) – Their 116 wins was still an MLB record through 2013, but they came up short in the World Series, losing to the in-town rival Chicago White Sox.

1934 St. Louis Cardinals (95–58) – The "Gashouse Gang," known for their shabby appearance and playing style, won the NL by two games and beat the Detroit Tigers in seven for the World Series.

1953 New York Yankees (99–52) – Hall of Famers such as catcher Yogi Berra, outfielder Mickey Mantle, and pitcher Whitey Ford capped an incredible five-year run of World Series titles.

1968 Detroit Tigers (103–59) – Cy Young and MVP Award winner Denny McLain helped Detroit win an MLB-best 103 games and the World Series title.

1973 Oakland Athletics (94–68) – Nicknamed the "Swingin' A's" because of their flashy personalities and offense, this team was the second of three consecutive title-winning teams in Oakland.

1986 New York Mets (108–54) – Young stars such as outfielder Darryl Strawberry and pitcher Dwight Gooden led the Mets to an MLB-leading 108 wins and the World Series.

1993 Toronto Blue Jays (95–67) – Outfield slugger Joe Carter capped off Toronto's second consecutive World Series title with a walk-off homer in the bottom of the ninth inning in Game 6 against the Philadelphia Phillies.

2001 Seattle Mariners (116–46) – This team won an AL-record 116 regular season games before losing the ALCS four games to one to the New York Yankees.

GLOSSARY

ace
The best starting pitcher on a team.

legend
A famous player who is remembered by fans.

pennant
A long, triangular flag. In baseball, the word is used to describe a league championship.

postseason
The playoffs in which the top teams from the regular season compete for a World Series title.

rookie
A first-year player in the major leagues.

sacrifice fly
When a batter hits a ball to the outfield that advances a base runner while giving up an out.

strike
A work stoppage by employees to protest conditions.

utility man
A player who plays multiple defensive positions.

FOR MORE INFORMATION

Further Readings

Rossman, Larry. *New York Yankees Then and Now*. San Diego, CA: Thunder Bay Press, 2013.

Sports Illustrated Kids Full Count: Top 10 Lists of Everything in Baseball. New York: Time Home Entertainment Inc., 2012.

Ward, Geoffrey C. *Baseball: An Illustrated History*. New York: Alfred A. Knopf, 2010.

Web Links

To learn more about MLB's best teams, visit ABDO Publishing Company online at **www.abdopublishing.com**. Web sites about MLB's best teams are featured on our Book Links page. These links are routinely monitored and updated to provide the most current information available.

INDEX

ABOUT THE AUTHOR

Alex Monnig is a freelance journalist from St. Louis, Missouri. He graduated with his master's degree from the University of Missouri in May 2010. During his career he has spent time covering sports events around the world, including the 2008 Olympic Games in China, the 2010 Commonwealth Games in India, and the 2011 Rugby World Cup in New Zealand.